COLLABORATION:
What Makes It Work

*A Review of Research Literature on Factors
Influencing Successful Collaboration*

Paul W. Mattessich, Ph.D.

Barbara R. Monsey, M.P.H.

Wilder Research Center, in association with
Wilder's Community Collaboration Venture

Amherst H. Wilder Foundation
St. Paul, Minnesota

This research summary was developed by Wilder Research Center, a program of the Amherst H. Wilder Foundation in Saint Paul, Minnesota. Wilder Research Center developed the report in collaboration with the Community Services Group—another Wilder program—that works in the Twin Cities metropolitan area to strengthen the capacity of individuals, organizations, and other groups to improve their communities.

The Amherst H. Wilder Foundation is one of the largest and oldest endowed human service agencies in America. For more than eighty years, the Wilder Foundation has provided human services responsive to the welfare needs of the community, all without regard to or discrimination on account of nationality, sex, color, or religious scruples.

We hope you find this report helpful! For information about other Foundation publications, please see the order form on the last page or contact:

Publishing Center
Amherst H. Wilder Foundation
919 Lafond Avenue
Saint Paul, MN 55104

Toll-Free 1-800-274-6024

If you have questions about the research, contact Paul W. Mattessich, Ph.D. or Barbara R. Monsey, M.P.H. at:

Wilder Research Center
1295 Bandana Boulevard North, Suite 210
Saint Paul, MN 55108

Phone (612) 647-4600

Researched and written by Paul Mattessich, Ph.D. and
   Barbara R. Monsey, M.P.H.
Designed by Rebecca Andrews

Manufactured in the United States of America

Library of Congress Catalog Card Number: 92-72633

ISBN 0-940-06902-4

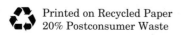
Printed on Recycled Paper
20% Postconsumer Waste

Contents

ACKNOWLEDGMENTS

Our work benefited greatly from the contributed talents and resources of others. Our funders (the Amherst H. Wilder Foundation, The Saint Paul Foundation, United Way of Saint Paul, United Way of Minneapolis, The Minneapolis Foundation) provided crucial underwriting of the work.

Michael Winer and Louise Miner have offered continued support, encouragement and stimulation during both the design and writing phases of manuscript development.

Within Wilder Research Center, Dan Mueller offered "quality control" by critiquing our methods. Frank Romero served on the project staff. Marilyn Conrad typed, formatted, and improved the manuscript. Rebecca Andrews designed the final layout.

Sharon Kagan provided both kind encouragement and wise advice on the content of this report and on the ways it can be useful to a broad range of readers. Dale Blyth offered valuable insight regarding the translation of research findings into practical implications. A number of other friends of the project reviewed manuscript drafts and offered helpful feedback: Audrey Anderson, Bryan Barry, Bruce Bobbitt, Sally Brown, Phil Cooper, Lucy Rose Fischer, Vince Hyman, Christine Jones and Gary Stern.

In the first stage of our work, a number of experts on collaboration (whose names appear in Appendix C) participated in lengthy interviews to provide us with leads, suggestions, and advice. In the last stage of our work, the participants at a conference "Collaboration Works," offered many useful ideas to make the final version of this report a better document.

To all of these individuals, we express our thanks! ■

PREFACE

The Wilder Foundation has a long-standing interest in the process of partnering among service-delivery agencies (the first Wilder publication to promote collaboration appeared in 1915). This project is a current example of that interest.

Publications of Wilder's Community Collaboration Venture include:
- This research-based report: *Collaboration: What Makes it Work*
- A practical step-by-step book: *Collaboration Handbook: Creating, Sustaining, and Enjoying the Journey* (see last page for ordering information).

Goals of this Report

1. To ***review and summarize*** the existing research literature on factors which influence the success of collaboration.

    We identified all research related to collaboration, screened out studies which didn't meet criteria for validity and relevance to collaboration, and combined the remaining set of studies to identify factors which influence success.

2. To ***report the results*** of the research literature review so that people who want to initiate or enhance a collaborative effort can benefit from the experience of others.

Methodology

The review and summary of research related to collaboration had three major stages. *First*, we identified all the research we could find related to collaboration. We searched through computer based bibliographies, contacted researchers interested in the topic, and tracked down bibliographic references in each document obtained. The scope of the search included the health, social science, education and public affairs arenas. From 133 studies examined, we screened out studies which were general "how-to" manuals, did not meet our definition of collaboration, or failed to meet other research criteria. After the screening, 18 studies remained.

Second, we carefully reviewed each of the 18 valid and relevant studies and identified factors which the studies reported as influencing the success of collaboration.

Third, we blended together the findings from the studies. We determined, for example, whether two researchers were using the same words to describe different factors, or different words to describe the same factor. As a result, 19 factors which influence the success of collaboration were identified. A detailed description of these procedures appears in **Appendix B**.[1]

After the research was completed, we presented the 19 factors at a conference on collaboration in the Twin Cities in May, 1992. Participants suggested interpretations and added to the implications section for each factor. ∎

---

[1] Wilder Research Center has now applied this type of method to analysis of literature in three domains: collaboration (this report); prevention programming (Mueller and Higgins, 1988); and productive aging (Fischer and Schaffer, in press).

Springfield saw a rise in youth problems. Many were not completing their education; some boys were turning to gang activities; and more single, young mothers entered the child protection and welfare system.

Leaders from the schools, nonprofit social service agencies, youth organizations, health agencies and government met to discuss how to make an impact upon the problems. Many agencies already provided services to teens, but many youth were falling through the cracks in the system.

After months of negotiation and discussion, the group applied for and received funding from a local foundation for a collaborative program within the schools for high risk teens. Agencies would provide services in the school setting such as health care and social service support. Springfield now anticipates a higher graduation rate, less delinquent behavior, healthier teens, and fewer teen pregnancies.

The Park Heights neighborhood was plagued by housing decay, transiency, absentee landlords and a lack of employment opportunities.

Neighborhood organizations came together with the schools, police, social service agencies and a neighborhood redevelopment agency to discuss what improvements might be made. Through the process of learning about each other and the different problems in the neighborhood, these groups joined together to start the Park Heights Neighborhood Initiative. The group now plans to develop goals and objectives for jointly improving the neighborhood.

Collaboration—An Effective Way to Work

Collaboration among human service, government, and community organizations has been around for years. But recently it's become a very hot topic. Why?

Pressure from funders, for one. Formal mandates and government initiatives are requiring many agencies to collaborate. The word is: autonomy and "going it alone" are frowned upon in complex systems such as mental health, services for the handicapped, and youth employment.[1]

But there's a less formal movement toward collaboration as well. A shrinking base of some traditional nonprofit resources has led many organizations to ask themselves if cost efficiencies could be possible by addressing common issues or delivering similar services together with their peers. Collaboration can reduce individual expenses in planning, research, training, and other development activities in the early stage of a new initiative. When overhead expenses are shared, duplication of cost and effort is avoided.

Collaboration—working together, rather than alone—interests an increasing number of people in human services, government, and community organizations.

Some funders have come to prize and promote it and evidence suggests successful collaborative efforts can produce very beneficial results.

Making services more accessible and effective is another potential benefit of collaboration. Helping people who have complex problems requires a great deal of coordination in order to provide the most efficient and effective assistance. Many organizations, in fact, now believe that the ability to get certain results can happen *only* through joint service efforts. Atelia Melaville and Martin J. Blank—researchers in the field of human service collaboration—emphasize that collaborative partnerships among human service agencies offer the ability to deliver services based on the *total* needs of clients—and the possibility of a truly integrated service system. A recent report, developed by the McKnight Foundation to describe its mid-point progress on an initiative to help families in poverty, stated:

> *Collaboration results in easier, faster and more coherent access*
> *to services and benefits and in greater effects on systems.*
> *Working together is not a substitute for adequate funding,*
> *although the synergistic efforts of the collaborating partners*
> *often result in creative ways to overcome obstacles.*[2]

---

[1] See, for example: P.L. 99-660, The U.S. Comprehensive Mental Health Services Planning Act; P.L. 99-457, Part H, Early Intervention Program for Handicapped Infants and Toddlers; Title IV, Part A, of the Youth Employment and Demonstration Projects Act, 1977; National Institute of Mental Health and The Rehabilitation Services Administration agreement of 1978; Minnesota Comprehensive Children's Mental Health Act. The State of Ohio mandates the "clustering" of children's services, in order to promote at least a minimal level of collaboration among agencies serving the same geographic area.

[2] See The McKnight Foundation (1991:21). Another foundation, the Annie E. Casey Foundation, has turned this principle into action by developing collaborative demonstration projects to address the needs of at-risk youth in four U.S. cities. See The Center for the Study of Social Policy (1991).

In her 1989 book, *Collaborating*, Barbara Gray notes that the quality of results often increases when a problem is addressed through interagency collaboration. This happens because organizations working jointly (rather than independently) are likely to do a broader, more comprehensive analysis of issues and opportunities. They also have complementary resources which "diversify" their capability to accomplish tasks. Arthur Himmelman—who has worked with collaborations in communities across the U.S.—points out in a recent article the great potential for collaborative activities to solve many difficult community problems.

Addressing the Key Questions

What are the ingredients of successful collaboration? What makes the difference between success and failure in joint projects? Collaboration—what makes it work?

Questions like these motivated the development of this report. We've tried to answer them by taking information from case studies about collaboration and putting it together in a readable format. We reviewed a vast amount of research, extracted the major findings, summarized them, and drew a few critical conclusions. We hope the resulting report offers important, accessible research material to anyone who wants to start a collaborative effort or better manage one in progress.

A Working Definition

The term collaboration is used in many ways and has a variety of meanings to different people. Here's our working definition:

> **Collaboration** *is a mutually beneficial and well-defined relationship entered into by two or more organizations to achieve common goals.*
>
> *The relationship includes a commitment to: a definition of mutual relationships and goals; a jointly developed structure and shared responsibility; mutual authority and accountability for success; and sharing of resources and rewards.*

In this report, we use ***collaboration*** to refer to the dynamic relationship defined above. We use the term ***collaborative group*** to refer to the set of organizations that join together in collaboration. The individuals who represent collaborating organizations are referred to as ***partners*** or ***members***.

A discussion of the working definition of collaboration appears in **Appendix A**.

A Theoretical Basis for Collaboration

Besides a definition, this report identifies and discusses 19 keys to success in collaboration. **What the report *doesn't* do is act as a guide to specific actions in your situation.** (The forthcoming collaboration workbook will provide step-by-step "how to" information.)

That's what we hope this report on collaboration will be for you: a source that illuminates the principles behind success and therefore provides insight into your own specific challenges.

Let's say this report focused on gardening—rather than collaboration. In that case we would inform you, as reader and prospective gardener, about the basics of growing a healthy, productive garden. For example, we'd talk about soil conditions, the length of the growing season, and how much sunlight and water is needed to grow various plants. We would not, however, offer detailed instructions on how to plan and tend your own garden.

You would have gained from our report a sound *theoretical* understanding of what gardens need in order to bear fruit; but you would still have to apply that theory in your own, real-world situation. That's what we hope this report on collaboration will be for you: a source that illuminates the principles behind success and therefore provides insight into your own specific challenges.

How to Use This Report

Perhaps you're a funding agency that's seeing increasing numbers of proposals for collaborative efforts, and need to know more about the subject. Maybe you're currently involved in a collaboration, and want some research results to back your hunches. Or maybe you'd just like some background information—a little homework on collaborations before you jump into one with your organization.

We hope that many people—program managers and planners, funders, policy-makers, and decision-makers in organizations large and small—will find it useful to have information on a set of key ingredients research says is key to collaborative success.

Here are some ways to put this report to work:

- For **general understanding:**
  Read the report to increase your knowledge of the success factors behind collaborative projects. You will then have a set of useful concepts

in mind when you consider collaboration as an option for achieving goals.

- In **specific situations:**

  Turn to the report when you need to plan or make a decision about a collaborative project. The material in Chapters Two and Three can serve you in at least three ways:

  1. Use the set of success factors as a checklist to determine if your group's plans include all necessary ingredients. If not, you can take steps to build in whatever the project lacks.

  2. Use the content of Chapter Three ("implications," discussion, and examples) to expand your thinking about ways to help your collaborative project succeed, comparing your situation with others that might be similar.

  3. After you have a collaborative effort underway, return to the material in the report to ask: What should we be watching out for? Are there changes we need to make in mid-course?

Chapter Four discusses the ways you can use this report in more detail. ∎

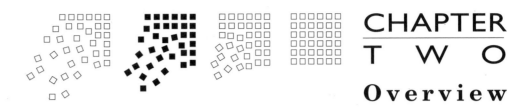

CHAPTER TWO
Overview

This chapter gives an overview of **19 factors that influence the success** of collaborations formed by human service, government, and other nonprofit agencies.

- The factors are grouped into six categories:

  1. Environment
  2. Membership
  3. Process/Structure
  4. Communications
  5. Purpose
  6. Resources

- Each factor from the research is listed, under its category, with a brief description. (The methods used to identify these factors are detailed in **Appendix B**.)

- Each factor has check marks assigned, indicating the number of studies which identified the factor as important to a collaboration's success.[1]

We wish to emphasize that the factors shouldn't be judged *solely* by the number of check marks they tallied. Research on collaboration is still in its early stages, and future studies may provide a better understanding of the true importance of each factor. The bottom line is: to ensure the effectiveness of your collaborative effort, pay attention to *all* the factors listed.

For more detail on each of the 19 factors, please see **Chapter Three**.

---

[1] *"Number of studies" is used to show relative importance (rather than a more quantitative measurement) because studies of collaboration are almost all case studies, with non-quantifiable data.*

Categories

1. Environment
2. Membership
3. Process/Structure
4. Communication
5. Purpose
6. Resources

Factors Influencing the Success of Collaboration

Number of Studies that Identify the Factor

1. Factors Related to the ENVIRONMENT

✓✓✓✓✓ **A. History of collaboration or cooperation in the community.**
A history of collaboration or cooperation exists in the community and offers the potential collaborative partners an understanding of the roles and expectations required in collaboration and enables them to trust the process.

✓✓✓ **B. Collaborative group seen as a leader in the community.**
The collaborative group (and by implication, the agencies in the group) is perceived within the community as a leader—at least related to the goals and activities it intends to accomplish.

✓✓✓ **C. Political/social climate favorable.**
Political leaders, opinion-makers, persons who control resources, and the general public support (or at least do not oppose) the mission of the collaborative group.

2. Factors Related to MEMBERSHIP CHARACTERISTICS

✓✓✓✓✓✓✓✓✓ **A. Mutual respect, understanding, and trust.**
Members of the collaborative group share an understanding and respect for each other and their respective organizations: how they operate, their cultural norms and values, limitations, and expectations.

✓✓✓✓✓✓✓✓✓ **B. Appropriate cross-section of members.**
The collaborative group includes representatives from each segment of the community who will be affected by its activities.

✓✓✓✓✓ **C. Members see collaboration as in their self-interest.**
Collaborating partners believe the benefits of collaboration will offset costs such as loss of autonomy and "turf."

✓✓✓ **D. Ability to compromise.**
Collaborating partners are able to compromise, since the many decisions within a collaborative effort cannot possibly fit the preferences of every member perfectly.

Factors Influencing Success　　　　　　　　　　　　　　*Number of Studies that Identify the Factor*

3. Factors Related to PROCESS/STRUCTURE

A. Members share a stake in both process and outcome.　　✓✓✓✓✓
Members of a collaborative group feel "ownership" of both the way the group works and the results or product of its work.

B. Multiple layers of decision-making.　　✓✓✓✓✓
Every level (upper management, middle management, operations) within each organization in the collaborative group participates in decision-making.

C. Flexibility.　　✓✓✓✓
The collaborative group remains open to varied ways of organizing itself and accomplishing its work.

D. Development of clear roles and policy guidelines.　　✓✓✓✓
The collaborating partners clearly understand their roles, rights, and responsibilities; and how to carry out those responsibilities.

E. Adaptability.　　✓✓✓
The collaborative group has the ability to sustain itself in the midst of major changes, even if it needs to change some major goals, members, etc., in order to deal with changing conditions.

4. Factors Related to COMMUNICATION

A. Open and frequent communication.　　✓✓✓✓✓✓✓
Collaborative group members interact often, update one another, discuss issues openly, convey all necessary information to one another and to people outside the group.

B. Established informal and formal communication links.　　✓✓✓✓
Channels of communication exist on paper, so that information flow occurs. In addition, members establish personal connections — producing a better, more informed, and cohesive group working on a common project.

Factors Influencing Success

5. Factors Related to PURPOSE

✓✓✓✓✓   **A. Concrete, attainable goals and objectives.**
Goals and objectives of the collaborative group are clear to all partners, and can realistically be attained.

✓✓✓✓   **B. Shared vision.**
Collaborating partners have the same vision, with clearly agreed upon mission, objectives and strategy. The shared vision may exist at the outset of collaboration; or the partners may develop a vision as they work together.

✓✓✓   **C. Unique purpose.**
The mission and goals or approach of the collaborative group differ, at least in part, from the mission and goals or approach of the member organizations.

6. Factors Related to RESOURCES

✓✓✓✓✓✓✓   **A. Sufficient funds.**
The collaborative group has an adequate, consistent financial base to support its operations.

✓✓✓✓✓✓   **B. Skilled convener.**
The individual who convenes the collaborative group has organizing and interpersonal skills, and carries out the role with fairness. Because of these characteristics (and others), the convener is granted respect or "legitimacy" from the collaborative partners. ∎

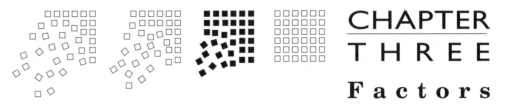

CHAPTER THREE
Factors

This chapter goes into more detail about each of the factors that influence the success of collaborations, as identified by the research literature.

Each entry includes:

A **description**: one to three sentences which explains the factor.

Implications: a discussion of the factor's practical importance for those who wish to start or enhance a collaborative effort. These suggestions are based upon our own analysis, using the observations of the original researchers as well as comments from readers of this report in its draft form.

Illustration: an excerpt from one of the research case studies.

Description

Implications

Illustration

I. Factors Related to the ENVIRONMENT

Environmental characteristics consist of the geographic location and social context within which a collaborative group exists. The group may be able to influence or affect these elements in some way; but it does not have control over them.

A. History of collaboration or cooperation in the community.

Description

A history of collaboration or cooperation exists in the community and offers the potential collaborative partners an understanding of the roles and expectations required in collaboration and enables them to trust the process.[1]

Implications

• Other things being equal, collaborative efforts will most likely succeed where cooperative or collaborative activity has a history or is encouraged.

• When planning a collaborative effort, goals should be set according to the level of development, understanding, and acceptance of collaboration within the community.

• If a major, new collaborative approach seems worthwhile even though a community has little or no history of collaboration, environmental issues should be addressed before starting the work. Examples include advocacy for legislation and/or funding which promotes collaboration, as well as educating potential collaborators regarding the benefits and processes of collaboration.

• Some parts of a community may provide an inhospitable environment for collaboration. For example, organizations may have a history of competitiveness.

Illustration

A 1990 study of 72 collaborative groups who provide child care and early childhood education offers an example of how the State of Florida has encouraged enduring collaborative relationships.[2]

---

[1] Note two things. First, "community" can have a clear geographic base; but it can also refer to a set of people or organizations with common ties based upon professional discipline, industry, ethnicity, etc. Second, the history of collaboration may not be of similar depth throughout a specific community. Organizations of certain types may have begun collaborative relationships long before organizations of other types.

[2] In each "Illustration" section in this chapter, case studies are referenced by the author's last name. Complete citations appear in the bibliography. In addition, Appendix D cross-references each study with each factor it identifies.

"While not free from challenges, Florida has demonstrated a long-term commitment to collaboration, never fully disbanding its Child Care Coordinating Councils. Given this historic legacy, collaborations [in child care] have been sustained throughout the state, fostering many local collaborations and the development of a state interagency cooperative agreement. Because of this long-standing commitment, Florida has been able to showcase exemplary collaborations to developing efforts, [sic] and knowledgeable leadership that had evolved at the local level was ready to assume broader responsibility as state initiatives expanded. While not the sole barometer of efficacy, a collaboration that is embedded in a historically and politically supportive context is more likely to survive than one that is not." (Kagan et al., p. 71)

B. Collaborative group seen as a leader in the community.

Description

The collaborative group (and by implication, the agencies in the group) is perceived within the community as a leader—at least related to the goals and activities it intends to accomplish.

Implications

- Collaborative groups which intend to make system-wide changes or work with the wider community must be perceived as a legitimate leader by the community they intend to influence.

- The early stage of a collaborative effort should include an assessment of the collaborative group's leadership image; and if deficient, the collaborative group should correct this image.

- Community-wide projects require broad legitimacy. Smaller scale projects will require legitimacy in the eyes of a narrower group.

Illustration

A 1992 study looks at a collaborative group in the garment industry who was applying for community development funds to start a job training program. The group found their poor reputation in the community posed a major barrier.

"In the past, the federal government's CETA program had regulations expressly precluding placement of workers in the sewing industry. The local economic development organizations believed that the 'fly by night' reputation was deserved so, consistent with theory, they saw no reason to help the garment industry. A major effort in this collaboration involved persuading these funding institutions that the garment firms in this collaboration were dependable corporate citizens." (Sharfman et al., p. 24)

C. Political/social climate favorable.

Description

Political leaders, opinion-makers, persons who control resources, and the general public support (or at least do not oppose) the mission of the collaborative group.

Implications

- Collaborating partners should spend time up front "selling the collaboration" to key leaders in order to create the best political climate possible.

- Often, the political and social climate acts as a positive external motivator to collaboration. For example, policymakers may encourage collaborations as a way of tackling issues most effectively.

- If the right climate does not exist, collaborating partners should consider strategies and tactics for improving the climate — changing public commitment, for example, to achieve the collaboration's goals.

- Collaborative groups should set goals realistically to meet political and social requirements.

- A collaborative group's goals and the process undertaken to reach those goals should be perceived as cost-effective and not in conflict with (or a drain on) ongoing community endeavors.[1]

- Beware that the political and social climate can change throughout the life of a collaborative group. Monitor and take action if the climate becomes negative.

Illustration

A 1991 study describes how collaborative groups working in the public policy arena used different strategies to develop a positive political climate.

"The general political climate, in the form of a public commitment to children by policymakers helped to gain support for policy development related to P.L. 99-457. This climate developed through the Governor's office and/or through the legislature. Some elected officials used a strategy of relating the need for early childhood programs to long term economic benefits for the state. We also observed that a favorable climate was often a function of influential parents and agency representatives putting children's issues on the policy agenda." (Harbin et al., p. 13)

---

[1] Neither of these last two implications is intended to imply that collaborative groups should never do anything which is politically controversial or which may lead to a revision in community priorities and/or funding patterns. Rather, they encourage strategic thinking on how to make collaborative effort as productive as possible within a specific set of social, historical, and political circumstances.

2. Factors Related to MEMBERSHIP CHARACTERISTICS

1	Environment
2	**Membership**
3	Process/Structure
4	Communication
5	Purpose
6	Resources

Membership characteristics consist of skills, attitudes, and opinions of the individuals in a collaborative group, as well as the culture and capacity of the organizations which form collaborative groups.

A. Mutual respect, understanding and trust.

Description

Members of the collaborative group share an understanding and respect for each other and their respective organizations: how they operate, their cultural norms and values, limitations, and expectations.

Implications

• At the very beginning of an effort, collaborating partners should temporarily set aside the purpose of the collaboration and devote energy to learning about each other.

• Partners must present their intentions and agendas honestly and openly to bring out trust-building.

• Building strong relationships takes time.

• Set aside time to understand cultural context and membership (how language is used, how people are perceived).

• Conflicts may develop due to a lack of understanding about the other partners in a collaborative group.

• Current connections through systems other than the proposed collaborative group provide a foundation for the communication, trust, and sharing that will be crucial to building a successful collaboration. If such connections do not exist, understanding why may be an important part of establishing the new group.

Illustration

A 1983 study of six interagency collaborative efforts points out the importance of respect for the boundaries, structure, procedures and processes of each organization in a collaborative group.

"There may be an elected chief executive, an elected legislative body, an elected commission, a governing body appointed by elected officials, a self-perpetuating private citizen board, an appointed executive staff, and civil service administrators, all needing to mesh their decision-processes. Decision-making and reporting procedures are quite different among say, a city council, a county department, a United Way board, or a large state bureaucracy. Important operations such as budget cycles, application formats, and reporting and monitoring procedures also differ by jurisdiction. United Way agencies normally operate on an annualized allocation process that begins after their fund drives. Local governments

have budget cycles that often differ from each other as well as from the state and federal governments. Foundations, on the other hand, tend to operate with less rigid time frames and have less structured application policies. Most of these units operate with their own reporting procedures, some monitor their funded programs whereas others do not. The six intergovernmental bodies studied did not attempt to integrate these various modes of operation into a single framework. To reach any solution, the differences have to be 'worked around,' with respect for, and willingness to work through, very different modes of operation." (Agranoff and Lindsay, p. 230)

B. Appropriate cross section of members.

Description

The collaborative group includes representatives from each segment of the community who will be affected by its activities.

Implications

- The group should carefully review who needs to be involved in the collaborative endeavor. They should take time to identify the people who have either explicit or unspoken control over relevant issues. These key people should be invited to become partners or to participate in the collaboration some other way.

- Partners should continuously monitor whether new groups or individuals should be brought into the ongoing process. A formal integration/education plan for new members should be developed.

- The cross-section of members cannot be so broad and the number of collaborative members so great that the process of collaboration becomes unmanageable.

- If agencies are similar in terms of purpose, areas served, characteristics of clients, the kinds of clients served, etc., they will already have some amount of understanding and interdependence upon which to build.

Illustration

A 1988 study reported on interviews of forty community leaders in Denver (some from The Denver Partnership and others who worked closely with the Partnership) about membership needs.

"They indicated the need to purposefully communicate with and cultivate relationships with the whole gamut of stakeholders, including officials of public agencies, newly-emerging as well as traditionally-involved civic and special interest groups, neighborhood groups and citizens." (Coe, p. 515)

C. Members see collaboration as in their self-interest.

Collaborating partners believe the benefits of collaboration will offset costs such as loss of autonomy and "turf." **Description**

- Make it very clear what member organizations stand to gain from the collaboration, and build those expectations into the goals so they remain visible throughout the life of the collaborative effort. **Implications**

- Build in incentives for individual organizations to get and stay involved. Monitor whether those incentives continue to motivate members.

A 1980 study of inter-institutional collaborations among education, employment and training organizations found that they worked best in settings where enlightened self-interest was present. **Illustration**

"With the other linkages, different factors provided incentives for cooperation. For example, the state housing authority saw an opportunity to utilize the expertise developed at the project to further some of its own goals. A ranking member of the housing authority has also been chosen to serve on the board of directors of the project. This was a major link for the future. The local neighborhood organization has received special housing services in return of their support of the project. The project has gained valuable on-the-job training experience as a result of the work provided by the organization." (Rist et al., p. 177)

D. Ability to compromise.

Collaborating partners are able to compromise, since the many decisions within a collaborative effort cannot possibly fit the preferences of every member perfectly. **Description**

- Participating organizations must give their representatives some latitude in working out agreements among partners. Rigid rules and expectations will render collaboration unworkable. **Implications**

- Collaborative members should allow time to act deliberately and patiently when reaching decisions.

- Collaborative members must know when to seek compromise or common ground and when to work through major decisions.

Illustration

A 1983 study describes how intergovernmental collaborative groups (with members from elected bodies, the voluntary sector and the public sector) moved forward slowly and deliberately in an effort to solve problems.

"Each group had to be prepared to accept less than an ideal solution to the problem but a course of action nevertheless. In many cases, the groups evolved into a 'two steps forward one step backward' mode to strengthen the structure. Three of the six bodies, for example, shifted from a comprehensive to problem-specific planning mode. The Dayton group began with a minimum capacity study of agencies, which it had to shelve for more immediate demands of elected officials. In Seattle, when the common data base project [its organizing issue] was deemed insurmountable, the group shifted to the solution of other problems." (Agranoff and Lindsay, p. 231)[1]

| 1 Environment |
| 2 Membership |
| **3 Process/Structure** |
| 4 Communication |
| 5 Purpose |
| 6 Resources |

3. Factors Related to PROCESS/STRUCTURE

Process/structure refers to the management, decision-making, and operational systems of a collaborative effort.

A. Members share a stake in both process and outcome.

Description

Members of a collaborative group feel "ownership" of both the way the group works and the results or product of its work.

Implications

- Adequate time and resources must be devoted to developing ownership among all participants in a collaborative effort.

- The operating principles and procedures of a collaborative group must promote among members a feeling of ownership about decisions and outcomes.

- Continuously monitor ownership of a collaborative group over time, and make needed changes in process or structure in order to ensure the feeling of ownership.

- Interagency work groups, participating in regular planning and monitoring of the collaborative effort, can solidify ownership and ongoing commitment.

---

[1] This illustration also offers a good example of adaptability (Factor 3E).

A 1983 study provides examples of how information sought through collaborative efforts is used by all partners.

Illustration

"Establishing and maintaining the involvement and active participation of major human service funders, elected officials, and administrators means the parties have a vested interest in the IGB [Intergovernmental Bodies] structure's existence and success. For example, all the IGBs use a wide base of funding to ensure that the parties have a vested interest in both the content of the problem-solving and the success of the project. The issues addressed were of recognized joint concern and provided benefits for the local community. Seattle's energy assistance project and Columbus' study of the effects of group homes on property values represent problems whose resolutions provided mutual benefits to the parties." (Agranoff and Lindsay, p. 232)

B. Multiple layers of decision-making.

Every level (upper management, middle management, operations) within each organization in the collaborative group participates in decision-making.

Description

- Successful collaborative groups recognize the multiple layers of management in each organization and create mechanisms to involve them.

Implications

- At the outset of collaboration, systems should be developed to include necessary staff from each organization.

- Linking leaders may not be sufficient to sustain a major collaboration. Integrating the efforts throughout all the members' systems builds stronger ties and probably greater success.

- It is important to have talented, key people in an organization assigned to work on the collaborative project and that they be interested in its success.

In a 1987 study of integrated services for pregnant and parenting teenagers, a structure developed for decision-making is described.

Illustration

"Leaders of each of the different components [education, day care, health, and counseling] meet as a group on a weekly basis. There is also an advisory committee which meets monthly to develop policy for the Mini School, provide advice and support, and help ensure adequate funding for program maintenance and expansion. The Advisory Committee includes a representative from each of the four agencies involved in the program plus representatives from other community groups which have interests in the ongoing operation and development of the program." (Holman and Arcus, p. 120)

C. Flexibility.

Description The collaborative group remains open to varied ways of organizing itself and accomplishing its work.

Implications • Collaborative groups need to be flexible both in their structure and in their methods.

• Communicating the need and expectation for flexibility is crucial at the outset of a collaborative effort.

• Monitoring the collaborative group to ensure it remains flexible is important, since groups often tend over time to solidify their norms in ways which constrain their thinking and their behavior.

Illustration A 1990 study of successful collaborations in the child care field provides examples of the kind of flexibility that is needed.

"It may be a flexible response to the collaboration's geographic environment (a collaboration in a rural, mountainous state holds meetings in alternative sections of the state to allow all members equal opportunity to attend at least half of the collaboration's meetings). It may be a creative way to address staffing shortages (a collaboration with local universities allows a child care agency to adequately staff its program with early education, nursing, social service, and food service students). It may be stretching resources to serve more than one purpose (a collaboration that receives corporate funding for its efforts to expand day care centers and homes to accommodate the needs of employees notes that this also increases the availability of child care for the public). Large accomplishments or small, collaborations report that flexible responses to their environment enable them to continue to pursue their goals." (Kagan et al., p. 43)

D. Development of clear roles and policy guidelines.

Description The collaborating partners clearly understand their roles, rights, and responsibilities; and how to carry out those responsibilities.

Implications • Members need to discuss the roles, rights, and responsibilities of the partners, reach agreement on these, and clearly communicate them to all relevant parties. Letters of agreement may be helpful.[1]

• Collaborating partners need to resolve any conflict resulting from demands placed upon them as employees of the organization they

---

[1] These could specify roles, rights, responsibilities, and procedures. They could also state the basic values and philosophy of the group. If possible, collaborating partners might have these letters developed and signed within every level of their organizations (see Factor 3B).

represent competing with demands they face as members of a collaborative team. Participating organizations may need to adjust policies and procedures to reduce this conflict in roles.

- Members' true interests and strengths should be considered when making assignments. Ultimately, people will gravitate towards their interest.

A 1990 study of interagency team development provides examples of how members of The Community Drug Team clarified roles and procedures.

Illustration

"In order to clarify roles, the team attempted to define profession-specific and generic skills and get agreement about who does what based on individuals in post. Recurring problems included the specific demands placed on some team members, such as the requirement of the probation officer to find acceptable placements, and appear before the court at short notice. Other members seemed more able to develop more long-term therapeutic commitments. Given that team members are also members of other teams, some degree of role conflict is also inevitable, and this required negotiation and agreement with the respective managers so that team activities were seen to contribute to professional responsibilities rather than act in competition with them."

"In order to clarify procedures the team agreed to record new referrals, arising through different routes, in a common referral book, and to allocate cases by agreement according to workload and case characteristics..." (Isles and Auluck, p. 161)

E. Adaptability.

The collaborative group has the ability to sustain itself in the midst of major changes—even changes of major goals or members—in order to deal with changing conditions.[1]

Description

- A collaborative group should keep itself aware of community trends, other changes in the environment, and the directions pursued by its members. It should accommodate itself to these developments.

Implications

- The vision and goals of a collaborative group must be reviewed regularly and revised if appropriate.

---

[1] Flexibility and adaptability may appear similar. However, they refer to two different aspects of a group process. Flexibility relates to means: the ability of a collaborative group to use different methods or structures, as needed, to meet the demands of a project. Adaptability relates to ends: the ability of a collaborative group to adjust its vision, fundamental goals, or philosophies as a result of new learnings or new conditions which have developed.

- Since member goals and outcomes change, collaborative goals and outcomes need to keep pace by continually incorporating changes as necessary.

Illustration   A 1990 study describes the adaptive process used by collaborative groups.

"While all the projects have in one manner or another implemented a school-to-work transition effort, it is also the case that, almost without exception, what now is in place is not entirely what was anticipated nor promised when the grant application was made. The process of improvisation and of continually readjusting the goals of the program to changing political, economic, and social conditions has resulted in efforts dissimilar to those initially envisioned." (Rist et al., p. xv)

| 1 Environment |
| 2 Membership |
| 3 Process/Structure |
| **4 Communication** |
| 5 Purpose |
| 6 Resources |

4. Factors Related to COMMUNICATION

Communication refers to the channels used by collaborative partners to send and receive information, keep one another informed, and convey opinions to influence the group's actions.

A. Open and frequent communication.

Description   Collaborative group members interact often, update one another, discuss issues openly, convey all necessary information to one another and to people outside the group.

Implications
- Set up a system of communication at the beginning of a collaborative effort, and identify the responsibilities each member has for communication.

- A staff function for communication may be necessary, depending upon the size and complexity of the collaborative group.

- Provide incentives within and among organizations to reward or highlight effective communication and discourage ineffective communications.

- Communications strategies must be planned to reflect the diverse communications styles of the members of the collaborative group.

- Acknowledge that problems will occur, and that they must be communicated. Acknowledge that conflict is good, and that there are topics on which collaborators may "agree to disagree."

- Avoid selective distribution of oral and written communication, since this might splinter the group.

A 1988 study of The Denver Partnership provides examples of how open communication increased the success of the collaborative groups. The Partnership established a transit/pedestrian retail mall and used frequent communication to strengthen relationships.

Illustrations

"To establish the district, business leaders carried a major leadership role. The approach included extensive collaboration, networking, and communication. Leaders met with other property owners and with elected and appointed public officials, circulated petitions, published notices in newspapers, and held informal meetings. Although boundaries were controversial, the property owners approved the district... The mile-long mall quickly became popular, attracting about 50,000 pedestrians and 40,000 shuttle bus riders per day and many more people dining, talking, resting, people-watching, or sunning in the various public spaces." (Coe, p. 508)

Another project of The Partnership, the development of a new convention center was not so successful, due in part to the lack of open communication.

"The convention center task force planning process was relatively closed, offering little opportunity for input by citizens (who believed they would bear the cost)... Communication with the community of interest was mainly one-way media communication, rather than networking or two-way communication. Opponents considered the project to be too heavily driven by business interests promoting their own welfare." (Coe, p. 511)

B. Established informal and formal communication links.

Channels of communication exist on paper, so that information flow occurs. In addition, members establish personal connections—producing a better, more informed, and cohesive group working on a common project.

Description

- Stable representation from collaborating organizations is needed to develop strong personal connections. If representatives "turn over" too rapidly, or differ from meeting to meeting, strong links will not develop.

Implications

- Communication efforts such as meetings, trainings, and interagency work groups should promote understanding, cooperation, and transfer of information.

- Setting aside purely social time might be helpful for members of a collaborative group.

- Review systems and procedures regularly to upgrade and expand communications.

- Don't rely too much on the paper process; get to know each other.

Illustration In a program where a number of agencies collaborated to provide educational, health, and social services to teen mothers, a 1987 study found that communication was improved by designating a particular staff person as liaison to the other members of the collaboration.

"Communication between these individual social workers and the other members of the Mini School team is facilitated by a Liaison Social Worker who has been assigned to the Tupper Mini School by the Ministry of Social Services and Housing. The Liaison Social Worker is an important link, helping to ensure that concerns and problems are dealt with quickly and that progress of both mother and child is communicated to all involved in the Mini School program. Without this link, it would be difficult to maintain the integrated approach which is a feature of the program." (Holman and Arcus, p.122)

| 1 Environment |
| 2 Membership |
| 3 Process/Structure |
| 4 Communication |
| **5 Purpose** |
| 6 Resources |

5. Factors Related to PURPOSE

Purpose refers to the reasons for the development of a collaborative effort, the result or vision the collaborative group seeks, and the specific tasks or projects the collaborative group defines as necessary to accomplish. It is driven by a need, crisis, or opportunity.

A. Concrete, attainable goals and objectives.

Description Goals and objectives of the collaborative group are clear to all partners, and realistically can be attained.

Implications
- Goals lacking clarity or attainability will diminish enthusiasm; clear, attainable goals will heighten enthusiasm.

- Collaborative groups must experience a progression of "successes" during the collaborative process in order to be sustained. Defining success too narrowly and distantly—only by accomplishing the collaboration's ultimate goals—can be discouraging.

- At the outset, collaborative groups should formulate clear goals, then periodically report on progress.

- Success will be more likely if a collaborative group develops both short- and long-term goals.

The six public/private collaborative projects in a 1983 study found success by focusing on concrete, attainable goals.

Illustration

"The focus on specific problems instead of contrived means of cooperation appears to be a particular keynote of success in these metropolitan areas. The real products of intergovernmental negotiations have been the solutions of problems considered important to the local actors. Concrete solutions, such as group home zoning ordinance, housing units for the mentally ill, the provision of emergency shelter for homeless persons, new types of classroom instruction, and increased access to services have been forthcoming." (Agranoff and Lindsay, p. 236)

B. Shared vision.

Collaborating partners have the same vision, with clearly agreed-upon mission, objectives and strategy. The shared vision may exist at the outset of collaboration; or the partners may develop a vision as they work together.

Description

- A collaborative group must develop a shared vision either when the collaboration is first planned, or just as it begins to function.

Implications

- Engage in vision-building efforts and develop a language and actions out of the shared vision.

- Technical assistance (outside consultation) may be useful to establish the common vision.

- Address openly any imbalances of power among collaborating partners. Make sure these imbalances do not stop the group from developing a truly shared vision.

A 1991 study of states who implemented coordinated services for families with a handicapped child discussed the importance of a shared vision.

Illustration

"A vision of the desired service system, which is shared by multiple persons in several centers of influence is critical to progress. Three of the six states studied had shared vision as an 'extremely strong' enabling factor. Progress also appeared to be related to the sharing of this vision across four to five agencies, organizations, power sources, and constituencies. An important part of the vision also is a set of administrative and political strategies by which the state can move from its current position to the desired vision." (Harbin et al., p. 11)

C. Unique purpose.

Description

The mission and goals or approach of the collaborative group differ, at least in part, from the mission and goals or approach of the member organizations.

Implications

- The mission and goals of a collaborative group must create a "sphere of activity." This sphere may overlap with but should not be identical to the sphere of any member organization.[1]

- The mission and goals of collaborative members need to be known by all involved.

- Collaboration among competing organizations to achieve goals each member already works toward may lead to failure. Less demanding attempts to coordinate or cooperate might fare better.

Illustration

In a 1988 study of The Denver Partnership, members were interviewed to determine successful ingredients in the multi-organizational setting.

"The respondents stressed the need for focus, avoiding provincialism but not overreaching geographically nor attempting an excessive number of tasks. They stressed that the organization should not attempt to usurp the responsibilities of others but recognize others' areas of responsibility and work within that framework." (Coe, p. 515)

1 Environment
2 Membership
3 Process/Structure
4 Communication
5 Purpose
6 Resources

6. Factors Related to RESOURCES

Resources include financial and human "input" necessary to develop and sustain a collaborative group.

A. Sufficient funds.

Description

The collaborative group has an adequate, consistent financial base to support its operations.

Implications

- Obtaining the financial means for existence must be a priority in forming a collaborative group.

- Collaborative work may be expensive in the start-up phase. Money should be available at the outset.

---

[1] Van de Ven (1976) suggests that an optimal range probably exists. The purpose of a collaborative group must be sufficiently close to the purpose of member organizations in order to make membership attractive. However, if it duplicates exactly the purpose of any member organization, that organization will not participate and may even attempt to subvert the collaboration.

- A collaborative group needs to consider the resources of its members as well as the necessity of approaching outside sources.

- In-kind support is as valuable as dollars.

A 1990 study of 72 successful collaborations around the country reports that 95 percent of the local-level collaborative groups have funding. Collaborations working for system changes in society have the most difficult time raising funds. The authors explain why this is such a serious problem.

"While these collaborations work to effect far-reaching change—a task requiring large commitments of time and attention from collaboration members—frequently, members of systems collaborations are distracted by the need to raise funds for their efforts. As the leader of one system collaboration stated, the group's existence is secure only for about six months at a time, when members must again become active in fund raising and grant writing." (Kagan et al., p. 37)

Illustration

B. Skilled convener.

The individual who convenes the collaborative group has organizing and interpersonal skills, and carries out the role with fairness. Because of these characteristics (and others), the convener is granted respect or "legitimacy" from the collaborative partners.

Description

- In selecting the collaborative group leader, care must be taken to find a person who has process skills, a good image, and knowledge of the subject area.

Implications

- Leaders of collaborative groups must give serious attention and care to their role.

- The grooming of new leaders and planning for transitions in leadership should be well-thought-out to avoid costly power struggles and loss of forward momentum.

- A convener should be skilled at maintaining a balance between process and task activities; and a convener should enable all members to maintain their roles within the collaborative group.

Key people in a collaborative group (particularly "lead agency" directors) need the skills and characteristics of a good leader, according to a 1991 study. The authors describe the critical skills for guiding the group.

Illustration

"(1) Being knowledgeable about state systems; (2) having previous experience with an interagency approach; (3) using participatory policy development style; (4) being informed about funding sources and systems; (5) having political skills that encourage actors such as legislators and the governor to support Part H; and (6) being able to take risks. We have found that a lead agency director, such as the director of special education programs, who is highly involved in providing vision and leadership contributes to progress in the development of policy." (Harbin et al., p.10) ■

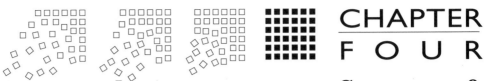

CHAPTER
F O U R

Summary &
Conclusions

We mentioned earlier that if our topic were gardening, the purpose of this report would be to identify the critical elements necessary for growing a healthy, productive garden. Chapters Two and Three might have identified factors such as levels of sunlight, water, air, or nutrients needed to produce a successful garden. Prospective gardeners could find out what "garden systems" require in order to thrive, and then apply their learning to the process of growing specific plants in specific sites. Some factors at those sites would come under the gardeners' complete control; but the gardeners would have little or no control over other factors.

As with gardens, successful collaborations require cultivation, and this report offers a guide to understanding the necessary ingredients for cultivating success.

To close, let's review and summarize what we have discussed, and how the information can be taken from here:

- Using the information
- The importance of the factors for your situation
    - *Are some more important than others?*
    - *What is the proper "mix" of factors?*
    - *Can a project succeed if it has most, but not all of the factors?*

Using the Information

We know that the readers of this report include:

Reader Profile

- Nonprofit and government agency managers and staff whose work draws them into collaborative situations with other organizations.

- Funders, policymakers, and other decision makers who need to allocate resources based upon the most cost-effective means to reach significant social goals.

- Others who work in, support, or advise collaborative groups.

We hope the report provides a theoretical understanding of the ingredients necessary for collaborative success. Individuals who want a thorough grounding in what makes collaboration successful can find it here; but you still need to decide on your own how to apply that knowledge.

For example, the research clearly indicates that mutual respect, understanding, and trust (Factor 2A) must develop among collaborators in order for their project to succeed. However, there are a variety of ways collaborators can go about developing and maintaining respect, understanding, and trust.

Ways to Use This Work

Let's elaborate on the uses of this report we talked about in Chapter One.

- For **general understanding:**
  Read the report to increase your knowledge of the success factors behind collaborative projects. You will then have a set of useful concepts in mind when you consider collaboration as an option for achieving your organization's goals.

  Some questions you might raise when you consider the option of collaborating with others to achieve a common goal:

  - Will it be possible, as best as you can estimate, to include all the factors necessary for success in your situation?

  - What will be the cost (time, money, other resources) of doing whatever it takes to make sure the success factors are included? Do the expected benefits of the collaboration exceed the potential costs?

- **In specific situations:**

  Turn to the report when you need to plan or make a decision about a collaborative project you're involved in. The material in Chapters Two and Three can serve you in at least three ways:

  1. Use the set of success factors as a checklist to determine if your group's plans include all necessary ingredients. If not, you can take steps to build in whatever the project lacks.

     Questions you might want to ask include:

     - How does a proposed project rate on each of the nineteen factors? For example, is there a history of collaboration or cooperation in the community (Factor 1A)? Do members see collaboration as furthering their self-interest (Factor 2C)?

     - If a proposed project rates low on a specific factor, is that a reason not to proceed; or can steps be taken to improve the rating?

     - Has the planning of a proposed project built in mechanisms for both *developing* and *sustaining* the factors necessary for the success of the collaborative group?

  2. Use the content of Chapter Three ("implications," discussion, and examples) to expand your thinking about ways to help your collaborative project succeed, comparing your situation with others that might be similar.

     For example, in order for members of a collaborative group to share a stake in both the process and outcome of their work (Factor 3A), Chapter Three suggests that adequate time must be devoted to the process of developing "ownership" among all participants in a collaborative effort. How will you build in that time?

  3. After you have a collaborative effort underway, return to the material in the report to ask: What should we be watching out for? Are there changes we need to make in mid-course?

     For example, you might find that you and the other collaborating partners did a good job building flexibility (Factor 3C) into your collaboration at the start. However, over time, members have slowly become more rigid; and this rigidity is decreasing your efficiency, if not your overall likelihood of success.

The Importance of the Factors for Your Situation

What is the proper "mix" of factors—can a project succeed if it has most, but not all of the factors?

Unfortunately, there is no simple answer to these questions. As a rough indicator of importance, Chapter Two showed the number of studies which identified each success factor. We suggested that the more studies identifying a factor, the greater the factor's influence in the success of collaborative projects.

With this in mind, recall from Chapter Two that the factors identified by the largest number of studies had to do with membership characteristics. This would imply that attributes and qualities of a collaborative efforts' members are more important than anything else when it comes to helping a collaboration succeed. Therefore, potential collaborators might conclude, they should concentrate most heavily on bringing the right partners together and building the right attitudes and spirit among them.

To go beyond this limited conclusion, you might recall our garden analogy. Sunlight is a factor necessary for a garden. If totally absent, the garden will not grow at all. However, if sunlight is present to some degree, the garden will still produce results.

As with the garden, it's likely that some benefits of collaboration can be achieved even if the success factors aren't present in ideal amounts. For example, if no trust exists among collaborators, the collaborative effort has about as much chance of succeeding as a garden without any sunlight. However, if partners at least minimally trust each other, they can probably reach many of their goals, even if they can't achieve as much as they would in a situation of very great trust. Keep in mind, too, that many factors are inter-related—building one may strengthen another. ■

AFTERWORD

Future Research

The factors identified in this research review need to be confirmed and quantified. We need to develop good measures of the factors; and we need to better define and measure what we mean by successful collaboration. Following-up on current collaborative efforts would produce many benefits. With good measurement techniques, this research would tell us how important each factor is, whether some are more important at certain stages than others, whether there is a "minimum required" level of any factor, and what the proper "mix" of factors is. How the factors relate to each other could also be explored. This research should also look at different types of collaborative groups to determine whether some factors are more important than others for specific types of groups.

It may also be useful to understand which of these factors are important for relationships of cooperation and coordination (see **Appendix A** for definitions of these relationships). Since these relationships are less intense and require less commitment, they might not require as many ingredients for success.

New research should look more closely at the history of specific collaborative efforts and how this history affects the importance of certain success factors. For example, are some factors more likely to be present in collaborative projects which are mandated than in projects which are completely voluntary? Is it more difficult to achieve certain factors in mandated collaborations? These are important questions if government, private funding agencies, and others decide to require collaboration as a condition of funding.

Research into the methods for building the factors into collaborative situations would have practical significance for potential collaborators. For example, there may be many ways to create a sense of ownership among participants; but which are most effective? Are some more effective than others with specific types of people or specific types of collaborative groups?

What about the "pre-collaborative" phase of relationships—the period before people approach one another and begin to work together? The research in this report covered collaboration after its initiation. What factors determine whether people will come together at all? Are they the same as the factors influencing collaborative success? Do other factors play an important role?

Finally, we need better research on the ***long-term outcomes*** of collaboration. Does collaboration really have any meaningful impact, for example, upon the people or communities whom the collaborating organizations serve? Even if the collaborating partners improve their situations through accomplishments such as relationship-building, capacity enhancement, or efficiency improvement, does the collaboration produce any long-term effects?

There is much to learn. Collaboration is a complex and powerful, yet often very fragile process. The work of many researchers who currently study this topic will greatly advance everyone's thinking about what is most crucial in the collaborative process. ■

Definition of Collaboration

Our working definition of collaboration is:

Collaboration *is a mutually beneficial and well-defined relationship entered into by two or more organizations to achieve common goals.*

The relationship includes: a commitment to: mutual relationships and goals; a jointly developed structure and shared responsibility; mutual authority and accountability for success; and sharing of resources and rewards.[1]

Defining collaboration is made complex by ambiguities in practical usage and scholarly disagreement about the term. In practice, 'collaboration' is commonly interchanged with 'cooperation' and 'coordination.' By contrast, the majority of scholars distinguish among cooperation, coordination, and collaboration.

Cooperation is characterized by informal relationships that exist without any commonly defined mission, structure or planning effort. Information is shared as needed, and authority is retained by each organization so there is virtually no risk. Resources are separate as are rewards.

Coordination is characterized by more formal relationships and understanding of compatible missions. Some planning and division of roles are required, and communication channels are established. Authority still rests with the individual organizations, but there is some increased risk to all participants. Resources are available to participants and rewards are mutually acknowledged.

Collaboration connotes a more durable and pervasive relationship. Collaborations bring previously separated organizations into a new structure with full commitment to a common mission. Such relationships require comprehensive planning and well defined communication channels operating on many levels. Authority is determined by the collaborative structure. Risk is much greater because each member of the collaboration contributes its own resources and reputation. Resources are pooled or jointly secured, and the products are shared.

---

[1] We are indebted to Michael Winer for his work on this definition. He combined the work of several experts to draft both the definition and the accompanying description of how collaboration differs from coordination and cooperation.

Cooperation, Coordination, & Collaboration
A Table Describing the Elements of Each [2]

Essential Elements	Cooperation	Coordination	Collaboration
Vision and Relationships	• basis for cooperation is usually between individuals but may be mandated by a third party • organizational missions and goals are not taken into account • interaction is on an as needed basis, may last indefinitely	• individual relationships are supported by the organizations they represent • missions and goals of the individual organizations are reviewed for compatibility • interaction is usually around one specific project or task of definable length	• commitment of the organizations and their leaders is fully behind their representatives • common, new mission and goals are created • one or more projects are undertaken for longer term results
Structure, Responsibilities & Communication	• relationships are informal; each organization functions separately • no joint planning is required • information is conveyed as needed	• organizations involved take on needed roles, but function relatively independently of each other • some project-specific planning is required • communication roles are established and definite channels are created for interaction	• new organizational structure and/or clearly defined and interrelated roles that constitute a formal division of labor are created • more comprehensive planning is required that includes developing joint strategies and measuring success in terms of impact on the needs of those served • beyond communication roles and channels for interaction, many 'levels' of communication are created as clear information is a keystone of success
Authority & Accountability	• authority rests solely with individual organizations • leadership is unilateral and control is central • all authority and accountability rests with the individual organization which acts independently	• authority rests with the individual organizations but there is coordination among participants • some sharing of leadership and control • there is some shared risk, but most of the authority and accountability falls to the individual organizations	• authority is determined by the collaboration to balance ownership by the individual organizations with expediency to accomplish purpose • leadership is dispersed, and control is shared and mutual • equal risk is shared by all organizations in the collaboration
Resources and Rewards	• resources (staff time, dollars and capabilities) are separate, serving the individual organizations' needs	• resources are acknowledged and can be made available to others for a specific project • rewards are mutually acknowledged	• resources are pooled or jointly secured for a longer-term effort that is managed by the collaborative structure • organizations share in the products; more is accomplished jointly than could have been individually

[2] *Adapted from the works of Martin Blank, Sharon Kagan, Atelia Melaville and Karen Ray*

The review and summary of research related to collaboration had three major stages:

1. Identification and Assessment of Research Studies
2. Systematic Codification of Findings from Each, Individual Study
3. Synthesis of Findings from Individual Studies

I. Identification and Assessment of Research Studies

A. Formulation of a Precise Research Question

In order to set both goals and parameters for the research review, a precise research question was required. This question was formulated as:

"What factors influence the success of collaborative efforts among organizations in the human services, government, and other nonprofit fields?"

This question oriented the work in several ways. It established that the research to be included in the review (the meta-analysis) must:

- Focus on collaboration.
- Have relevance for the collaboration which occurs among human services, government and other nonprofit organizations.[1]
- Relate to the success of a collaborative endeavor (measured in terms of outcomes)—not merely to the reasons for collaboration, the process, or other features.

B. Collection of Potentially Relevant Studies

Research staff then searched for and collected all pieces of work which were reported to be "collaboration research." The search occurred through: computerized bibliographic searches in the areas of social science, health, education, and public affairs; personal inquiries to researchers known for their interest in the topic, to obtain both their work and references to the work of others; and the tracking down (in a snow ball fashion) of bibliographic references appearing in materials as they were gathered.

These activities led to the acquisition of references to 133 studies.

---

[1] Note that this requirement does not mean that all studies had to involve organizations in these fields, only that the results had to be relevant to these organizations. In point of fact, most, but not all, of the studies reviewed in this report involved human service, government, or other nonprofit organizations.

C. Development of Acceptance Criteria

Meta-analytic research reviews require the establishment of criteria by which every potential study for inclusion in the final analysis is determined to be acceptable or unacceptable.

For the collaboration research review, research staff established that a study had to meet the following criteria for inclusion in the review:

1. The study must address the major research question (as described above).

2. The joint organizational effort analyzed by the study must meet the definition of "collaboration" developed for this research project. That is, it must truly be a *collaborative group,* not merely a loose cooperative or coordinated arrangement.[1]

3. The study must address the topic of success of the collaborative group.

4. The study report must include some sort of specific, empirical observations. It could not merely represent the "thoughts" of an expert; nor could it merely contain generalizations based upon "broad experience."

5. The study must be sufficiently translated into English, if it was not originally reported in English.

D. Initial Screening of Potentially Relevant Studies

Brief information was obtained for as many of the 133 studies as possible. This included abstracts and summaries which enabled the research staff to assess the probable worth of a particular study, based upon a very liberal application of the acceptance criteria listed above. For each research study estimated to have probable worth, research staff attempted to obtain a complete report from the study. These reports came in the form of journal articles, formally published reports, and informally published (or typically unpublished) reports.

This screening reduced the number of potential studies to 62.[2]

E. Critical Assessment of Studies

For each of the complete studies in hand, researchers made a critical assessment of the study's ability to meet the acceptance criteria for inclusion in the research review. At this point, the criteria were very strictly applied. Studies were dropped because they did not address the major research question adequately; the projects did not meet our

---

[1] See **Appendix A** for the definition of collaboration and its differences from other forms of joint efforts.

[2] 36 studies were dropped from consideration because they failed to meet the acceptance criteria; 35 were dropped because complete study reports could simply not be obtained.

definition of collaboration; they did not include empirical observations; or they did not address the topic of success.

This assessment reduced the number of studies to 18.

2. Systematic Codification of Findings from Each, Individual Study

A. Development of a Methodology

The central research question asked for the identification of factors which influence the success of collaboration. A typical meta-analysis would pool all the empirical studies which analyzed the relationship between a specific factor and collaborative success. Based upon this pooling, a result would emerge, identifying the importance, if any, of the factor.[1]

The problem with research on collaboration is that virtually every study employs only a case study methodology, not detailed empirical methods. Case studies are not amenable to the pooling of quantifiable data.

Therefore, we needed to develop a way to:

- Identify the success factors that each case study demonstrated.
- Indicate the weight or importance of each factor as an influence upon success.

The primary methodological rules developed for culling success factors from case studies were that:

1. The case study must include a statement by the case researcher that a particular factor is something which influenced the success of the collaborative group which was studied.

2. It must be possible for an outside observer (in this case, a WRC researcher) to link the statement by the case researcher about the factor directly to evidence in the case study of its effect upon success.

Even within a review of empirical research studies, this can be a difficult task; but in working with case studies, it becomes a monumental challenge.[2]

---

[1] For good overviews of the process of meta-analysis, see: Rosenthal, 1991; Altman, 1990; Light and Pillemar, 1984. For a discussion of some of the challenges facing meta-analysts, see Iyengar (1991).

[2] Rosenthal (1991:13) insightfully observes, for example, that by "research results" we "do not mean the conclusion drawn by the investigator, since that is often only vaguely related to the actual results. The metamorphosis that sometimes occurs between the results section and the discussion section is itself a topic worthy of detailed consideration. For now, it is enough to note that a fairly ambiguous result often becomes quite smooth and rounded in the discussion section, so that reviewers who dwell too much on the discussion and too little on the results can be quite misled as to what actually was found."

B. Identification of Factors

A WRC researcher carefully reviewed each study, identifying factors which were stated in the study to influence success and which could be linked to study evidence.

C. Validation of Factors

A second WRC researcher independently reviewed each of the case studies and critically examined each factor identified by the first researcher to validate that it met the two criteria listed in (A).

3. Synthesis of Findings from Individual Studies

A. Determining the List of Factors

The list of factors from individual studies was examined. In some cases, the wording of factors in two or more studies was identical; and they could easily be counted as the same. In other cases, the wording differed slightly. In these cases, two researchers looked closely at the factors and their associated case studies and decided whether the factors were the same. Where they could come to a firm decision on whether two factors were the same, their decision stood. When they could not make a firm decision, a third researcher was asked to review the factors; and the three researchers reached consensus. Two factors which were identified by only one study each were dropped from the list.

This process led to the identification of 19 factors from the combined findings of 18 studies.[1]

B. Tallying the Importance of Factors

For the final list of factors, the number of studies which cite each factor was tallied. The result provides a rough estimate of the importance of a factor or its weight in influencing collaborative success. Case study results cannot provide quantified estimates beyond this; future research on collaboration could do so (if it becomes more quantitative).

C. Putting the Factors into Categories

For ease of presentation, discussion, and use, the factors were placed into six categories. There is no research significance to the category groupings or to their names. If users of the report feel that a different grouping is appropriate, they can develop new categories without compromising the basic meta-analytic work. ■

---

[1] All factors are stated in the "positive," even though studies may have stated their "negative" dimension or indicated that the lack of the factor produced failure.

Collaboration Experts Interviewed

Bryan Barry
Wilder Foundation
Services to Organizations
919 Lafond Avenue
St. Paul, MN 55104

Ruth Belzer
The Harris Foundation
Two North LaSalle Street, Suite 605
Chicago, IL 60602-3703

Renee Berger
Director of Team Works
1117 North 19th Street, Suite 900
Arlington, VA 22209

Martin Blank
Senior Associate
The Institute for Educational
    Leadership, Inc.
1001 Connecticut Ave. NW, Suite 310
Washington, DC 20036

Dave Brown
Institute for Development Research
20 Park Plaza, Suite 1103
Boston, MA 02116-4399

Cheryle Casciani
Annie E. Casey Foundation
31 Brookside Drive
Greenwich, CT 06830

Louis Delgado
John and Katherine T. MacArthur
    Foundation
140 South Dearborn Street
Chicago, IL 60603

D. D. (David) Dill
University of North Carolina-Chapel
    Hill, South Building
Chapel Hill, NC 27514

Sheri Dodd
Joining Forces
400 North Capitol St. NW, Suite 379
Washington, DC 20001

Barbara Gray
Penn State University
College of Business Administration
Dept. of Mgmt. and Organization
408 Beam Business Admin. Building
University Park, PA 16802

Dr. Gloria Harbin
Caroline Institute for Child and Family
    Policy
Univ. of North Carolina-Chapel Hill
300 NCNB Plaza
Chapel Hill, NC 27514

Shirley Hord
Southwest Educational
    Development Lab
211 East Seventh
Austin, TX 78701

John Johnson
950 Pershing Circle
Burnsville, MN 55437

Sharon L. Kagan
Bush Center for Child Development and
    Social Policy
Box 11A, Yale Station
New Haven, CT 06520

Karen Ray
Suite 4315
12500 Marion Lane
Minnetonka, MN 55343

Cheryl Rogers
Senior Research Associate
Center for the Study of Social Policy
1250 Eye Street NW, Suite 503
Washington, DC 20005

Linda Silver
Wilder Foundation
Community Care Resources
919 Lafond Avenue
St. Paul, MN 55104

Gene Urbain
Parent Outreach Project
Wilder Foundation
919 Lafond Avenue
St. Paul, MN 55104

APPENDIX D

Author/ Factor Matrix

This chart cross-classifies each factor with each study which identified it. Studies are listed alphabetically by author's names. Full citations appear in the bibliography.

	Alaszewski and Harrison 88	Agranoff and Lindsay 83	Auluck and Isles 91	Bierly 88	Coe 88
1. Factors Related to the Environment					
A. History of collaboration or cooperation in the community.				●	
B. Collaborative group seen as leader in the community.					●
C. Political/social climate favorable.					
2. Factors Related to Membership Characteristics					
A. Mutual respect, understanding, and trust.		●	●	●	●
B. Appropriate cross section of members.		●		●	●
C. Members see collaboration as in their self-interest.		●			
D. Ability to compromise.		●			
3. Factors Related to Process/Structure					
A. Members share a stake in both process and outcome.		●			●
B. Multiple layers of decision-making.	●	●			●
C. Flexibility.		●			
D. Development of clear roles and policy guidelines.					
E. Adaptability.		●			
4. Factors Related to Communication.					
A. Open and frequent communication.	●	●	●	●	●
B. Established informal and formal communication links.				●	
5. Factors Related to Purpose					
A. Concrete, attainable goals and objectives.		●		●	●
B. Shared vision.					
C. Unique purpose.					●
6. Factors Related to Resources					
A. Sufficient funds.	●	●			
B. Skilled convener.					

Davidson 76	Hackstaff-Goldis, & House 90	Harbin et al 91	Harrison et al 90	Hodson et al 76	Holman and Arcus 81	Horwitch and Prahalad 81	Iles and Auluck 90	Kagan et al 90	McCann and Gray 86	Means et al 91	Rist et al 80	Sharfman, et al 91
●		●		●				●			●	
											●	●
		●						●	●			
	●	●	●				●			●	●	●
		●	●	●	●	●		●	●		●	
●									●	●	●	●
●					●							
		●	●		●	●						
			●		●						●	
			●					●			●	
●			●				●				●	
						●					●	
		●	●		●		●					
					●	●		●			●	
			●								●	
		●						●		●	●	
					●			●				
		●		●	●			●	●	●		
●		●	●			●		●	●			●

Alaszewski, Andy and Larry Harrison

1988　"Literature Review: Collaboration and Co-ordination between Welfare Agencies." ***British Journal of Social Work*** 18:635-647.

Altman, Lawrence

1990　"New Method of Analyzing Health Data Stirs Debate." ***New York Times,*** August 21, 1990, p. B5.

Agranoff, Robert and Valerie Lindsay

1983　"Intergovernmental Management: Perspectives from Human Services Problem Solving at the Local Level." ***Public Administration Review*** May/June:227-237.

Auluck, Randhir and Paul Iles

1991　"The Referral Process: A Study of Working Relationships Between Antenatal Clinic Nursing Staff and Hospital Social Workers and Their Impact on Asian Women." ***British Journal of Social Work*** 21:41-61.

Bierly, Eugene W.

1988　"The World Climate Program: Collaboration and Communication on a Global Scale." ***The Annals*** 495:106-116.

Center for the Study of Social Policy

1991　"The New Futures Initiative: A Mid-Point Review." Washington, D.C.: Center for the Study of Social Policy.

Coe, Barbara

1988　"Open Focus: Implementing Projects in Multi-Organizational Settings." ***International Journal of Public Administration*** 11(4):503-526.

Davidson, Stephen

1976　"Planning and Coordination of Social Services in Multiorganizational Contexts." ***Social Service Review*** 50:117-137.

Fischer, Lucy Rose, and Kay Schaffer

In
Press　***Older Volunteers: A Guide to Research and Practice***

Gans, S.P., and G.T. Horton
1975   "Integration of Human Services." New York: Praeger.

Gray, Barbara
1989   *Collaborating*. San Francisco: Jossey-Boss.

Hackstaff-Goldis, Lynn and Susan T. House
1990   "Development of a Collaborative Geriatric Program Be-
        tween the Legal System and a Social Work-Directed Pro-
        gram of a Community Hospital." *Social Work in Health
        Care* 14(3):1-16.

**Harbin, Gloria, Jane Eckland, James Gallagher, Richard Clifford
and Patricia Place**
1991   "Policy Development for P.L. 99-457, Part H: Initial Find-
        ings from Six Case Studies." Carolina Institute for Child
        and Family Policy, University of North Carolina, Chapel
        Hill, NC.

**Harrison, Patrick J., Eleanor W. Lynch, Kendra Rosander
and William Borton**
1990   "Determining Success in Interagency Collaboration: An
        Evaluation of Processes and Behaviors." *Infants and
        Young Children* 3(1):69-78.

Himmelman, Arthur
1990   "Community-Based Collaborations: Working Together for a
        Change." *Northwest Report* November, 1990, p. 26.

Hodson, Norma, Mary Ann Armour and John Touliatos
1976   "Project Uplift: A Coordinated Youth Services System."
        The Family Coordinator 25 (3): 255-260.

Holman, Nicole and Margaret Arcus
1987   "Helping Adolescent Mothers and Their Children: An
        Integrated Multi-Agency Approach." *Family Relations*
        36(2):119-123.

Horwitch, Mel and C.K. Prahalad
1981   "Managing Multi-Organization Enterprises: The Emerging
        Strategic Frontier." *Sloan Management Review*
        22(2): 3-16.

Isles, Paul and Randhir Auluck
1990   "Team Building, Inter-agency Team Development and Social Work Practice." ***British Journal of Social Work*** 20: 165-178.

Iyengar, Satish
1991   "Much Ado About Meta-Analysis." ***Chance: New Directions for Statistics and Computing***. 4(1) 33-40.

Kagan, Sharon L.
1991   ***United We Stand: Collaboration for Child Care and Early Education Services.*** New York: Teachers College Press.

Kagan, Sharon L., Ann Marie Rivera and Faith Lamb Parker
1990   "Collaboration in Practice: Reshaping Services for Young Children and Their Families." The Bush Center in Child Development and Social Policy, Yale University.

Light, Richard J., and David B. Pillemer
1984   ***Summing Up: The Science of Reviewing Research.*** Cambridge, Massachusetts: Harvard University Press.

McCann, Joseph E., and Barbara Gray
1986   "Power and Collaboration in Human Service Domains." ***International Journal of Sociology and Social Policy*** 6(3):58-67.

The McKnight Foundation
1991   ***The Aid to Families in Poverty Program,*** Minneapolis, Minnesota: The McKnight Foundation.

Means, Robin, Lyn Harrison, Syd Jeffers, and Randall Smith
1991   "Co-Ordination, Collaboration and Health Promotion: Lessons and Issues from and Alcohol/Education Programme." ***Health Promotion International*** 6(1):31-39.

Melaville, Atelia, with Martin J. Blank
1991   "What It Takes: Structuring Interagency Partnerships to Connect Children and Families with Comprehensive Services." Washington, D.C.: Education and Human Services Consortium.

Mueller, Daniel, and Paul Higgins

1988   *Funders' Guide Manual: A Guide to Prevention Programs in Human Services,* St. Paul: Wilder Foundation.

Rist, Ray C, Mary Agnes Hamilton, Wilfred B. Holloway, Steven D. Johnson, and Heather E. Wiltberger

1980   "Patterns of Collaboration: The CETA/School Linkage, An Analysis of Inter-Institutional Lilnkages Between Education and Employment/Training Organizations." Interim Report #4, Youthwork National Policy Study, Cornell University, Ithica N.Y.

Rosenthal, Robert

1991   *Meta-Analytic Procedures for Social Research.* Newbury Park, California: Sage.

Sharfman, Mark P., Barbara Gray and Aimin Yan

In Press   "The Context of Interorganizational Collaboration in the Garment Industry: An Institutional Perspective." *Special Issue on Collaboration in The Journal of Applied Behavior Science.*

Van de Ven, Andrew

1976   "On the Nature, Formation, and Maintenance of Relations Among Organizations." *Academy of Management Review* 4:24-36. ■

ABOUT THE AUTHORS

Paul W. Mattessich, Ph.D., is director of Wilder Research Center, which conducts research related to human services trends, programs and policies. Mattessich has been involved in applied social research since 1973, and is the author or co-author of more than 100 publications and reports. He has also served on a variety of task forces in government and the nonprofit sectors. He received his Ph.D. in Sociology from The University of Minnesota.

Barbara R. Monsey, M.P.H., is a research associate at Wilder Research Center and editor of the newsletter, *Findings*. Monsey has formal training in anthropology and a master's degree in Public Health Education from the University of North Carolina.

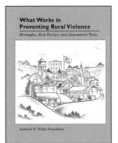